AMAZING ANIMALS
CROCODILES

BY VALERIE BODDEN

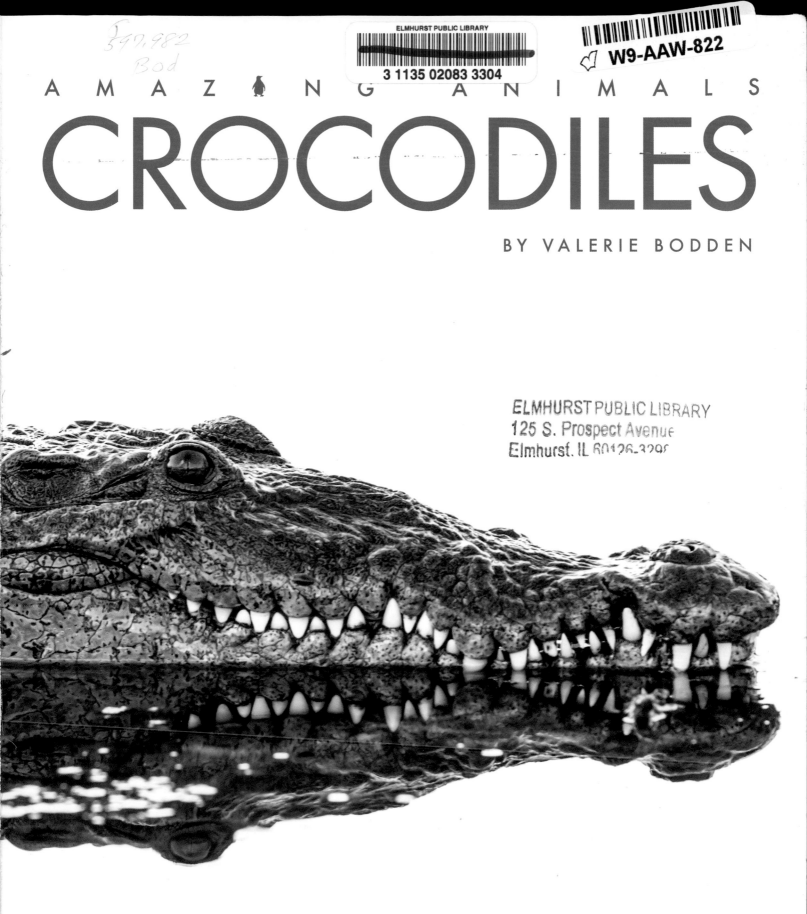

CREATIVE EDUCATION • CREATIVE PAPERBACKS

Published by Creative Education and
Creative Paperbacks
P.O. Box 227, Mankato, Minnesota 56002
Creative Education and Creative Paperbacks are
imprints of The Creative Company
www.thecreativecompany.us

Design by The Design Lab
Production by Angela Korte and Colin O'Dea
Art direction by Rita Marshall
Printed in the United States of America

Photographs by Alamy (Reinhard Dirscherl, Water-
Frame), Getty Images (Shaen Adey, James Hager, Art
Wolfe), iStockphoto (270770, ANDREYGUDKOV,
Paul Clarke, ed78, johan63, Jurie Maree, roborigi-
nal, StuPorts), Minden Pictures (Suzi Eszterhas)

Library of Congress Cataloging-in-Publication Data
Names: Bodden, Valerie, author.
Title: Crocodiles / Valerie Bodden.
Series: Amazing animals.
Includes bibliographical references and index.
Summary: This revised edition surveys key aspects of
crocodiles, describing the swimming reptiles' appear-
ance, behaviors, and habitats. A folk tale explains
why these creatures have rough, bumpy skin.
Identifiers: ISBN 978-1-64026-201-0 (hardcover)
/ ISBN 978-1-62832-764-9 (pbk) / ISBN 978-1-
64000-326-2 (eBook)
This title has been submitted for CIP processing under
LCCN 2019937901.

CCSS: RI.1.1, 2, 4, 5, 6, 7; RI.2.2, 5, 6, 7, 10;
RI.3.1, 5, 7, 8; RF.1.1, 3, 4; RF.2.3, 4

First Edition HC 9 8 7 6 5 4 3 2 1
First Edition PBK 9 8 7 6 5 4 3 2 1

Table of Contents

The skin on a crocodile's underbelly is soft but tough.

Crocodiles are big reptiles.

They spend much of their time in water. There are 14 kinds of crocodiles in the world. Some live in salty water. Others live in fresh water.

reptiles animals that have scales and a body that is always as warm or as cold as the air around it

Many crocodiles form groups called basks or floats.

 in sidebar

CROCODILES

7

Crocodiles are long. Their bellies are wide. Their **snouts** and tails are pointy. Crocodiles are covered with tough, bumpy skin. The skin is tan, brown, gray, or green. Some crocodiles have black patches.

snouts the projecting parts of animals' faces that include the nose and mouth

Some crocodiles are very big. Saltwater crocodiles are the biggest. Nile crocodiles are usually about 16 feet (4.9 m) long. Other crocodiles are smaller. Dwarf crocodiles are only about five feet (1.5 m) long. They weigh less than 100 pounds (45.4 kg).

Some crocodiles weigh more than three grown-up men put together.

Crocodiles use their powerful tails to leap out of the water.

Crocodiles live in warm, watery places around the world. They live along the banks of rivers and the shores of lakes. They live in wetlands, too.

wetlands areas of low-lying land that are covered with water

Crocodiles eat meat.

Their strong jaws are lined with sharp teeth. But they cannot chew. They swallow food whole. Crocodiles snap up small animals such as birds and fish. They hunt big animals, too.

Crocodiles will eat anything they can catch—including wildebeest (above)!

Young crocodiles have dark markings that fade with age.

A mother crocodile lays lots of eggs. She stays close to the nest. The eggs **hatch** after one to three months. Baby crocodiles are smaller than a ruler. Animals like eagles hunt them. They stay close to their mother for up to two years. Those that survive may live more than 50 years.

hatch to break open and produce a young animal

Crocodiles cannot

sweat. If they are hot, they open their mouths or lie in the shade. They may go in the water to cool down, too. If they are cold, they move to a spot in the sun.

Big crocodiles do not face threats from other animals.

Crocodiles can swim up to
25 miles (40.2 km) per hour.

Crocodiles spend a lot of time swimming. They wave their strong tail back and forth. This pushes them through the water. Sometimes they swim with just their eyes and **nostrils** above the water. They can swim under the surface, too. Some can stay underwater for two hours.

nostrils holes in the nose used for breathing and smelling

Today, some people watch crocodiles in the wild. From the safety of a boat, people can see crocodiles swim and hunt silently. It is exciting to see these big reptiles in action!

A crocodile's tail is about half its total length.

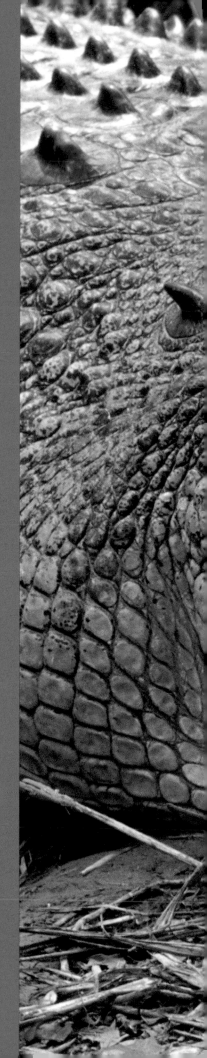

A Crocodile Tale

People in Africa used to tell a story about why crocodiles have rough skin. They said that the crocodile came out only at night. Because of this, he had smooth skin. But then the other animals said they liked the crocodile's skin. The crocodile was proud. He came out during the day to show off his skin. Soon, the sun made the crocodile's skin rough and bumpy. It stayed that way!

Read More

Gagne, Tammy. *Crocodiles: Built for the Hunt.* North Mankato, Minn.: Capstone Press, 2016.

Meister, Cari. *Do You Really Want to Meet a Crocodile?* North Mankato, Minn.: Amicus, 2015.

Terp, Gail. *Is It an Alligator or a Crocodile?* North Mankato, Minn.: Black Rabbit Books, 2020.

Websites

ELS: Crocodile Games
https://www.eslgamesplus.com/crocodile-games/
Practice vocabulary and grammar while playing crocodile games.

Enchanted Learning: Alligators and Crocodiles
https://www.enchantedlearning.com/themes/alligator.shtml
This site has alligator and crocodile activities and coloring pages.

National Geographic Kids: Amazing Animals Episode 39
https://kids.nationalgeographic.com/videos/amazing-animals/#crocodile.mp4
Learn more about crocodiles, the world's largest reptiles!

Note: Every effort has been made to ensure that the websites listed above are suitable for children, that they have educational value, and that they contain no inappropriate material. However, because of the nature of the Internet, it is impossible to guarantee that these sites will remain active indefinitely or that their contents will not be altered.